THE NATURE KIDS GUIDE TO

ELK

DAVID ANDERSON

LP Media Inc. Publishing
Text copyright © 2026 by LP Media Inc.
All rights reserved.

For information address LP Media Inc. Publishing,
30012 Variolite St NW, Princeton MN 55371
www.lpmedia.org

Publication Data

Elk
The Nature Kid's Guide to Elk — First edition.

Summary: "Learn all about Elk, the Nature Kid Way"
— Provided by publisher.

ISBN: 979-8-89818-147-5

[1. Elk – Non-Fiction] I. Title.

Title: The Nature Kid's Guide to Elk

CONTENTS

MOUNTAIN MEADOWS

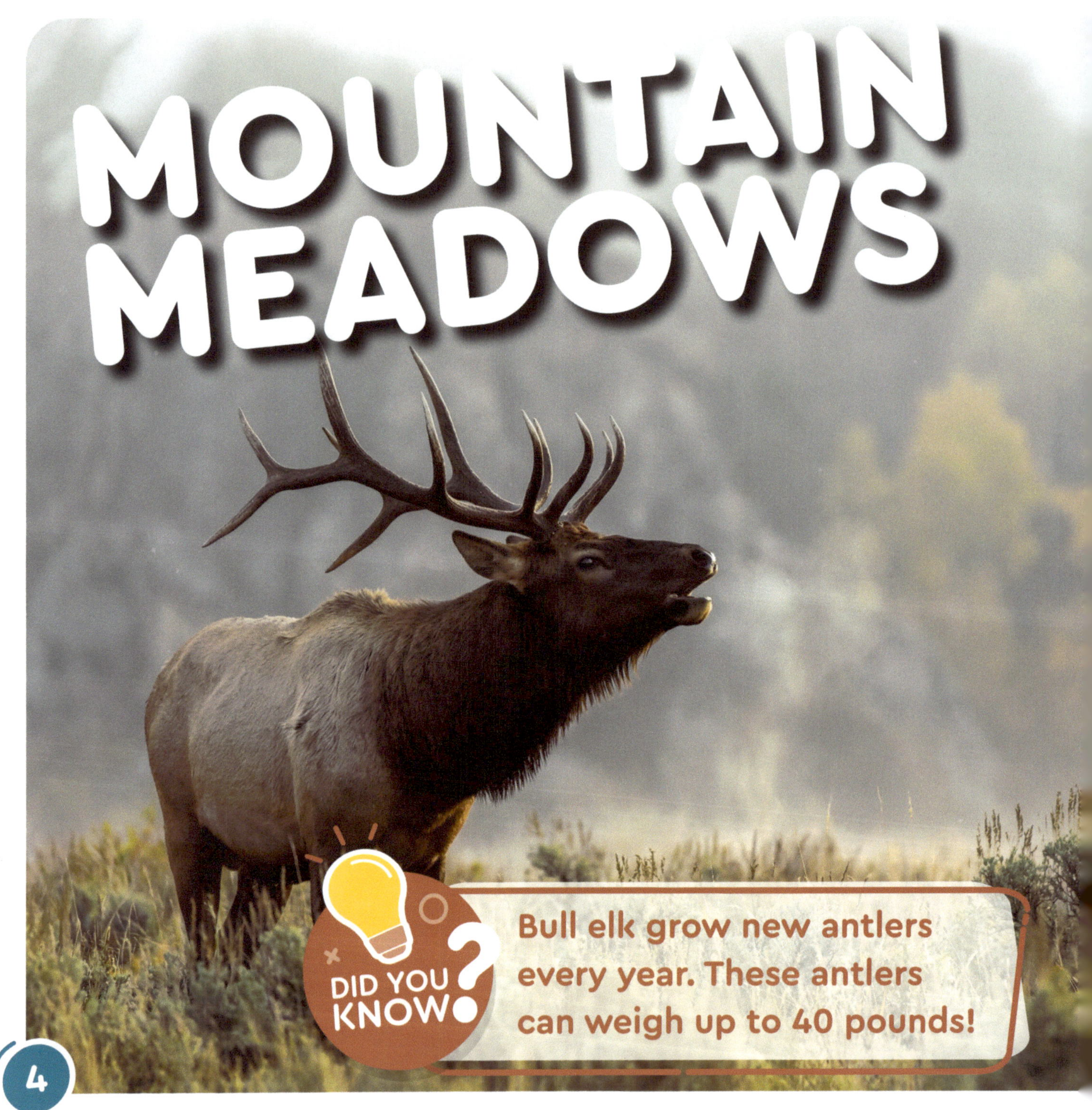

Bull elk grow new antlers every year. These antlers can weigh up to 40 pounds!

Bugle! A bull elk calls across a meadow. His voice echoes in the mountains.

Elk live in forests and mountains across western North America. They especially like open meadows and grassy valleys.

Elk need large home ranges of up to 10,000 acres to roam. They move between forests and open fields. In summer, elk climb to elevations up to 10,000 feet where the cool mountain air feels good.

In winter, elk come down to lower valleys. The snow is not as deep there, so they can find grass to eat. Elk also need fresh water and drink up to 4 gallons a day!

ELK EVERYWHERE

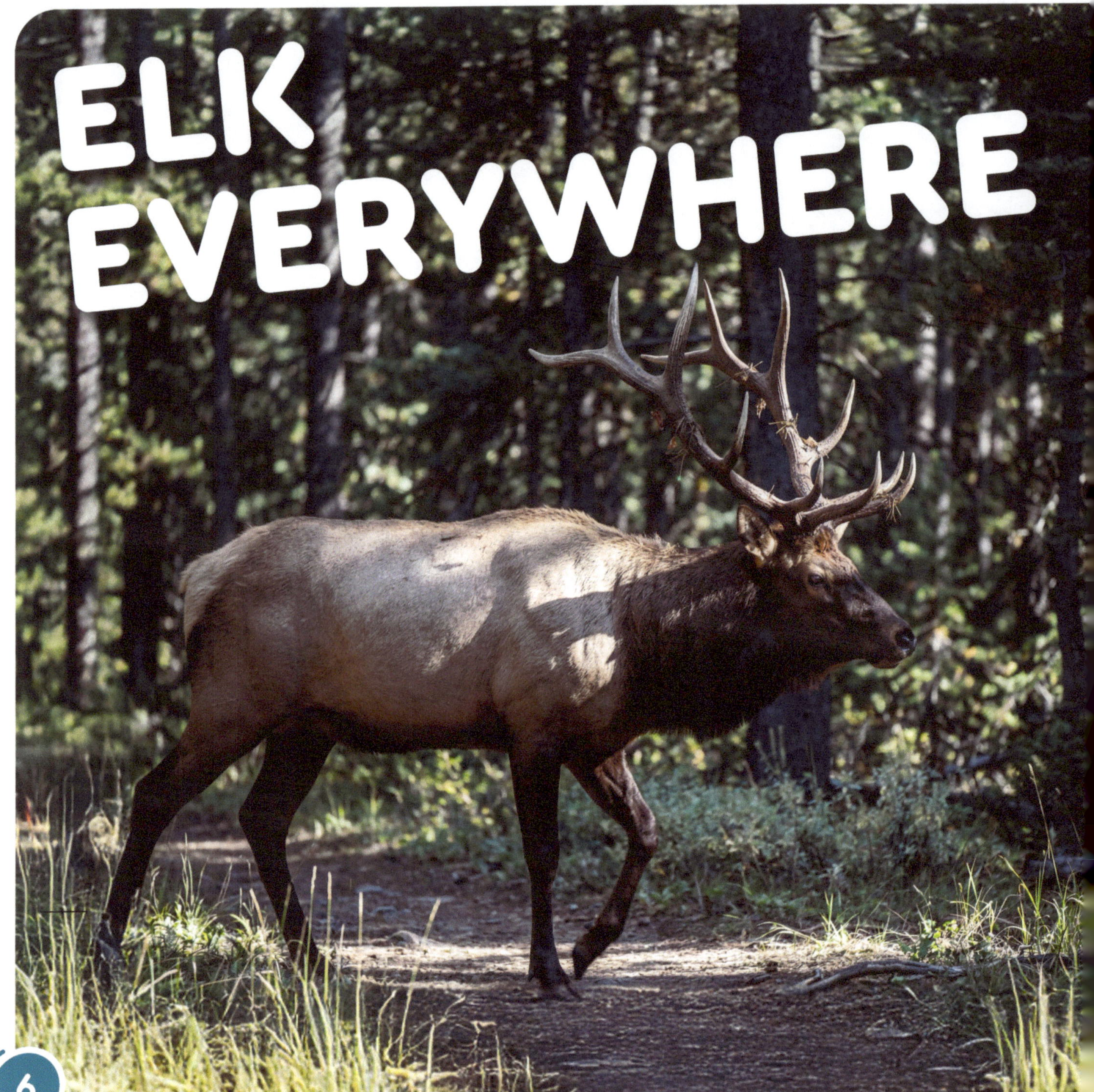

Thump! An elk's hooves hit the forest floor as it walks through the trees.

Elk once roamed across most of North America. They lived from coast to coast. Today, most elk live in the western United States and Canada.

Different types of elk live in different places. Rocky Mountain elk are found in Colorado and Wyoming. Roosevelt elk live in the rainy Pacific Northwest.

Elk have been reintroduced to many eastern states. You can even see elk in the Great Smoky Mountains!

Elk once lived in almost every U.S. state. By 1900, only 100,000 remained.

SUPER
SIZED

Stomp! A huge elk walks by. It is taller than a horse!

Elk are one of the largest deer in the world. A bull elk can stand 5 feet tall at the shoulder. That is as tall as many adult humans. With their antlers they can measure up to 9 feet tall!

Bull elk weigh between 700 and 1,100 pounds. Cows are smaller, weighing 500 to 600 pounds.

An elk's body can be 8 feet long from nose to tail. Their long legs help them run fast.

A newborn elk calf weighs about 35 pounds. It grows fast in its first year!

AWESOME ANTLERS

Crack! Two bull elk clash antlers. Their racks smash together.

Only male elk grow antlers. These massive racks can weigh up to 40 pounds!

Elk antlers grow fast. They can grow one inch per day in spring and summer. Soft skin called **velvet** covers the growing antlers. This velvet brings blood to help antlers grow.

In late summer, the velvet dries and falls off. The antlers underneath are hard bone. Bull elk shed their antlers in late winter. Then new ones grow back each spring.

A bull elk's antlers can stretch 4 feet wide!

SNIFF AND
SCAN

Sniff! An elk lifts its nose high. It smells the air.

Elk have a strong sense of smell. Their large noses can detect scents from far away. This helps them find food and sense danger.

Elk also have great hearing. Their big ears can turn in different directions, even two different ways at once!

Elk eyes sit on the sides of their heads. This lets them see almost all the way around without having to move their heads very far.

Elk can smell a wolf from up to a mile away! Their noses have 297 million scent receptors.

BUILT TOUGH

**Grunt! A bull elk lowers his head.
His thick neck muscles flex.**

Elk have tough bodies that help keep them safe. Their thick skin and dense fur protect them from bites and scratches.

Bull elk have thick necks with extra muscle. This helps protect them during fights with other bulls.

Elk also have strong, sharp hooves. They can kick **predators** with great force. A kick from an elk can break bones!

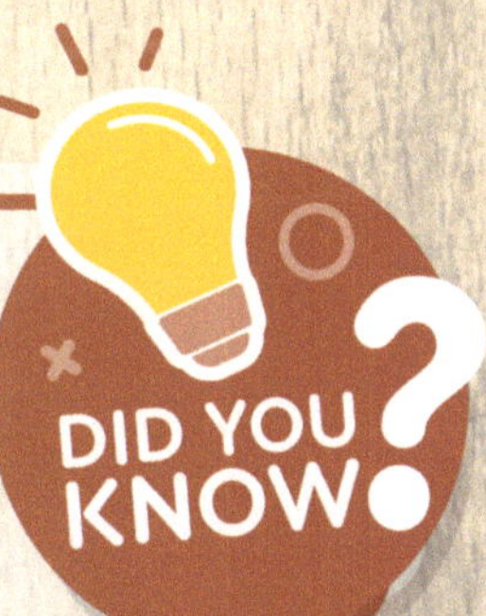

Elk skin is so tough that Native Americans used it to make shields and armor.

GRASSY
GRUB

Crunch! An elk bites off a mouthful of grass. It chews slowly.

Elk are **herbivores**. This means they only eat plants. They spend many hours each day eating.

Grasses are their favorite food. Elk also eat shrubs, tree bark, and leaves. In summer, they munch on wildflowers too.

Elk have special stomachs with four parts. This helps them digest tough plants. They swallow food, then bring it back up to chew again. This is called chewing **cud**.

An elk can eat up to 30 pounds of food a day!

BUGLE CALL

A bull elk's bugle call sounds like a high-pitched whistle, and can be as loud as a lawn mower!

FUN FACT!

A bull elk throws back his head. He calls out loud.

Elk make many sounds to talk to each other. The most famous is the **bugle**. Bull elk bugle the most, but cow elk can bugle too. This call starts low, rises high, then ends with grunts.

Bulls bugle most in fall. The sound tells other bulls to stay away. Bugles can be heard from up to two miles away!

Cow elk make different sounds. They use high chirps and barks. Mothers call to their calves with soft mews. Calves answer back with squeaks.

Elk also use body language. They raise their heads to show strength.

WATCH OUT

Howl! A gray wolf howls in the morning light. It's tracking an elk.

Elk have several predators. A wolf pack can have up to 37 members. They work together to catch one.

Mountain lions also hunt elk. These big cats hide and wait. They pounce from rocks or trees.

Bears sometimes catch elk too. Grizzly bears can run up to 40 miles per hour. This speed helps them catch young or sick elk. Black bears also hunt elk, mostly catching calves in spring.

Mountain lions can leap 40 feet in a single bound to catch their prey!

RUN FAST

FUN FACT!
Elk can jump up to 8 feet high. They leap over fences and logs to escape danger.

Whoosh! An elk sprints across a field. Its long legs move so fast they blur.

Elk are fast runners. They can reach speeds of 45 miles per hour. This helps them escape danger.

When elk sense a predator, they use their speed and long legs to get away. They can run through rough, rocky ground that slows wolves and bears down.

Elk also stay in groups for safety. Many eyes watching means predators are spotted sooner.

Calves can stand within 30 minutes of being born. Being fast keeps the whole family safe.

ON THE GO

Splash! An elk wades across a river. Water drips from its legs.

Elk are built for endurance. They can trot for hours without getting tired. Their long legs help them travel many miles each day.

Elk walk, trot, and run. They can keep up a steady trot of 10 to 20 miles per hour for a long time. This helps them move between meadows and forests to find food.

Elk are also strong swimmers. Their hollow hair helps them float well in water.

Elk can travel up to 50 miles a day when migrating between summer and winter ranges!

25

DAY BY DAY

Rustle! An elk grazes in the early morning light. The forest is waking up.

Elk are most active at dawn and dusk. They spend these cool hours eating and moving around.

During the hot middle of the day, elk rest. They find shady spots in forests, which helps them save energy.

At night, elk may sleep or graze. They take short naps throughout the day and night, usually resting for 30 minutes to an hour at a time.

Elk can doze while standing up! Their legs lock in place so they can rest without falling over.

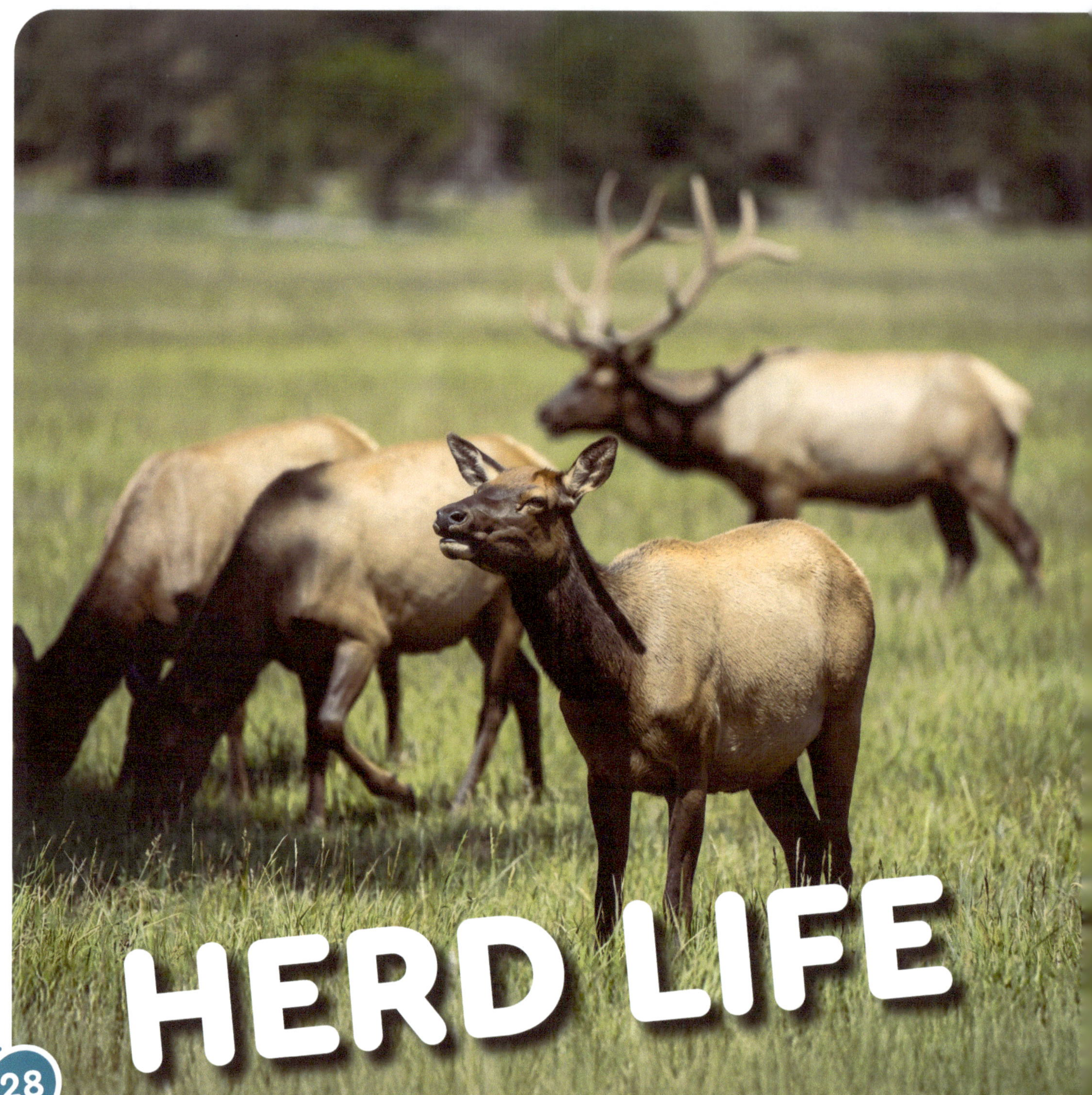

HERD LIFE

Snort! A cow elk looks up. Her herd grazes nearby.

Elk live in groups called herds. Cows and calves stay together all year. Bulls join them in fall.

Herds can have 200 or more elk. An older cow leads the herd. She decides where the group will travel and when to move to new feeding grounds.

In winter, herds gather in valleys. There, they share the best feeding spots.

When danger strikes, one elk barks a loud alarm. The whole herd can flee in just 2 seconds!

FALL FIGHTS

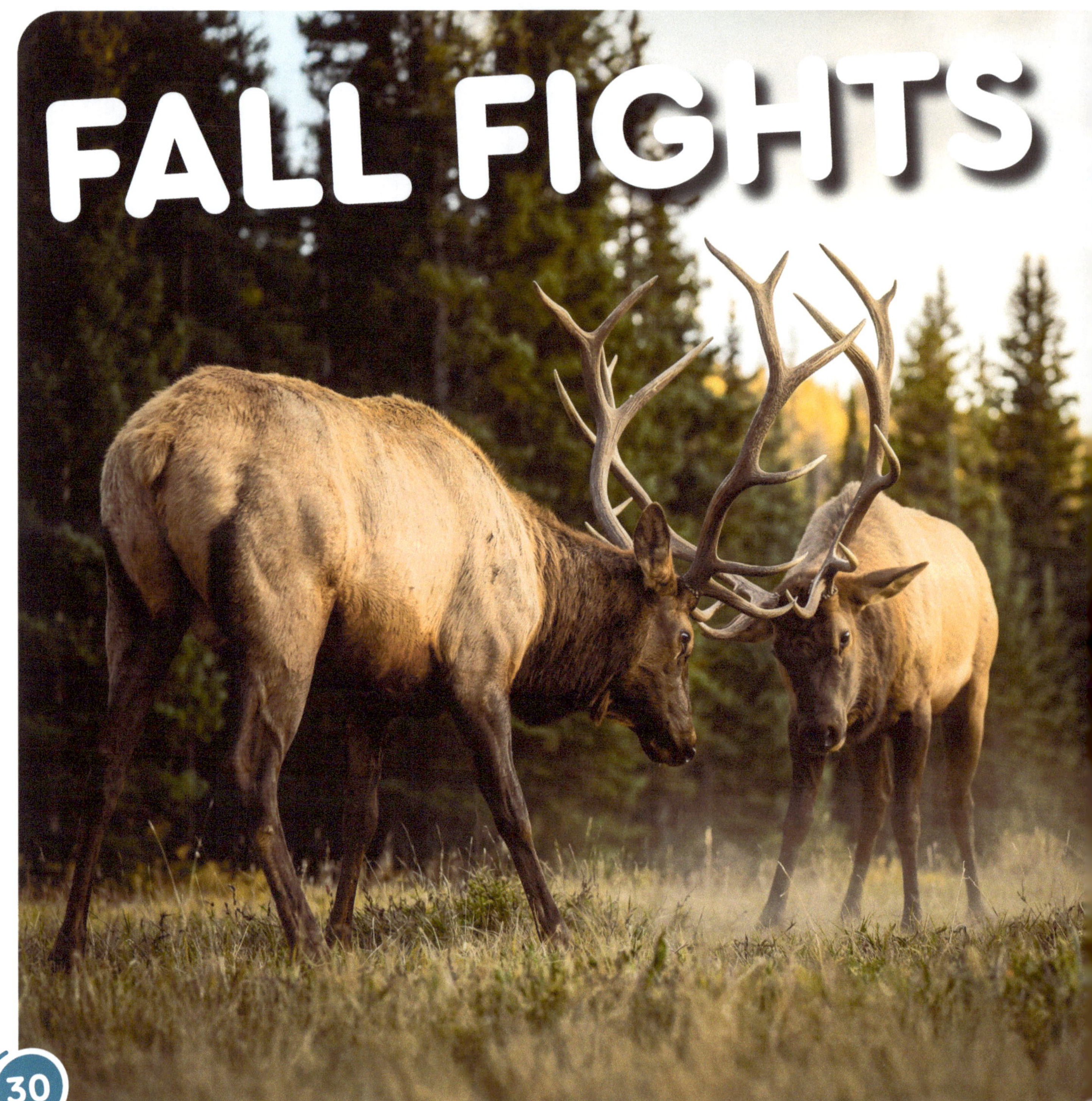

Clash! Two bull elk fight in a meadow. Their antlers crash like thunder.

Fall is mating season for elk. Bulls compete for cows by pushing and shoving with their antlers.

Before fighting, bulls often walk side by side to show off their size. Then they lock antlers and push hard. The stronger bull usually wins.

Most fights last only a few minutes. The losing bull walks away, and the winner stays with the cow herd.

Bull elk can lose 200 pounds during mating season. They barely eat or sleep for weeks!

CUTE CALVES

DID YOU KNOW?
Elk calves lose their spots by the end of summer. Their coats turn solid brown like adult elk.

Grunt! A baby elk calls for its mother. She comes running.

Baby elk are called calves. They are born in late spring. Most calves weigh about 35 pounds at birth.

Newborn calves have spotted coats. The white spots help them hide in tall grass. This makes it hard for predators to see them.

Calves can stand within 20 minutes of being born. They start walking soon after. Then, by two weeks old, they can run fast enough to keep up with the herd.

MOM KNOWS

Swoosh! A mother elk nudges her calf. She guides it to safety.

Cow elk are caring mothers. They protect their calves from danger. A calf stays close to its mother for about one year.

Mothers hide their newborns in tall plants. They visit several times a day to feed them milk. While mom is away, the calf stays still and quiet.

Cow elk teach their calves important skills. They show them where to find food and water. By following their mothers, calves learn to survive.

A mother elk can recognize her own calf's cry among hundreds of others!

THRIVING TODAY

Rumble! A herd of elk crosses a wide valley. These strong animals thrive.

Long ago, elk almost disappeared. People hunted too many. By the early 1900s, only about 50,000 elk were left. So laws were made to protect elk.

Elk are doing well today. About one million elk now live in North America.

Now elk live in many parks and forests. People work hard to keep their homes safe.

Yellowstone National Park is home to seven different elk herds. In summer, 10,000 to 20,000 elk roam the park

ELIK SPOTTING

Click! A camera snaps a photo. An elk poses in the wild.

Many people love watching elk. National parks are great places to see them. Look for elk in open meadows near forests.

The best times to spot elk are dawn and dusk. On cloudy days, they may stay out longer. In fall, listen for bulls bugling! Bring binoculars to see them up close.

Always stay at least 25 yards away. These wild animals need space. Watch quietly and enjoy!

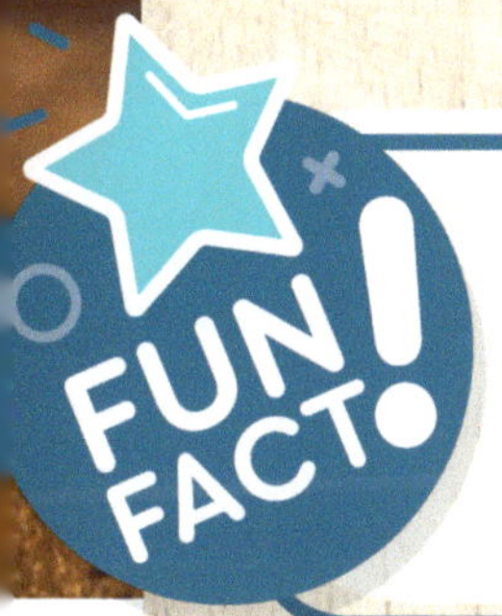

Elk watching causes 'elk jams' - traffic backups when visitors stop to take photos!

GLOSSARY

herbivores
Animals that only eat plants, not meat.

velvet
Soft, fuzzy skin that covers and helps grow an elk's antlers.

cud
Food that an animal swallows, then brings back up to chew again.

bugle
A loud, high call that elk make to talk to each other.

predators
Animals that hunt and eat other animals.